¡Puedo ser lo que quiera! / I Can Be Anything!

PUEDO SER CHEF
I CAN BE A CHEF

Miller Slenzak

Traducido por / Translated by Eida de la Vega

Gareth Stevens PUBLISHING

Please visit our website, www.garethstevens.com. For a free color catalog of all our high-quality books, call toll free 1-800-542-2595 or fax 1-877-542-2596.

Library of Congress Cataloging-in-Publication Data

Names: Slenzak, Miller, author.
Title: I can be a chef = Puedo ser chef / Miller Slenzak.
Description: New York : Gareth Stevens Publishing, [2019] | Series: I can be anything! = ¡Puedo ser lo que quiera! | Includes index.
Identifiers: LCCN 2017045286| ISBN 9781538227305 (library bound)
Subjects: LCSH: Cooking–Vocational guidance–Juvenile literature.
Classification: LCC TX652.4 .S545 2019 | DDC 641.5023–dc23
LC record available at https://lccn.loc.gov/2017045286

First Edition

Published in 2019 by
Gareth Stevens Publishing
111 East 14th Street, Suite 349
New York, NY 10003

Translator: Eida de la Vega
Editorial Director, Spanish: Nathalie Beullens-Maoui
Editor, English: Kate Mikoley
Designer: Laura Bowen

Photo credits: Cover, p. 1 (kid) Andy-pix/Shutterstock.com; cover, p.1 (background) Tyler Olson/Shutterstock.com; pp. 5, 11, 23 wavebreakmedia/Shutterstock.com; p. 7 Roman Kosolapov/Shutterstock.com; p. 9 Gorodenkoff/Shutterstock.com; pp. 13, 24 Kondor83/Shutterstock.com; pp. 15, 24 otnaydur/Shutterstock.com; p. 17 Rawpixel.com/Shutterstock.com; pp. 19, 24 OkFoto/Shutterstock.com; p. 21 Evgeny Litvinov/Shutterstock.com.

Printed in the United States of America

CPSIA compliance information: Batch #CS18GS: For further information contact Gareth Stevens, New York, New York at 1-800-542-2595.

Contenido

Contents

¡Los chefs cocinan comidas deliciosas!

Chefs cook yummy food!

Los chefs trabajan
en restaurantes.
Estos son lugares donde
la gente come.

They work in restaurants.
These are places
where people eat.

Trabajan en la cocina.
Ahí es donde se hace
la comida.

They work in a kitchen.
This is where food
is made.

Algunos usan gorros grandes.

Some wear big hats.

Usan cacerolas y sartenes.

They use pots and pans.

También usan un horno.

They also use an oven.

Los chefs hacen el menú.
El menú es la lista de
la comida.

Chefs make the menu.
This is the list of food.

Menu
Starter
Goat Cheese Salad
Tuscan Garden Salad
Main
Salmon with Lemon and Butter Sauce
Baby Rack of Lamb
with Fresh Herbs and Spices
Dessert
White Chocolate Cheesecake
Passion Fruit Cake
Homemade

Mi tía es chef.
Ella hace pasta.

My aunt is a chef.
She makes pasta.

Algunos chefs hacen pasteles.

Some chefs make cake.

Puedo ser chef.
¡Y tú también!

I can be a chef.
So can you!

Palabras que debes aprender
Words to Know

(el) horno
oven

(la) pasta
pasta

(la) cacerola
pot

Índice/Index